EARTH SCIENCE

Introduction to Weather

PAMELA BLISS

PICTURE CREDITS
Cover background: © Kevin Schafer/Corbis; page 1 (bkgd) © Taxi/Getty Images;
page 2 (bkgd) © Jay Dickman/Corbis; page 4 (bkgd) © Creatas; page 6 (bkgd)
© Corel Professional Photos; page 7 (top right) © Julie Eggers/Bruce Coleman,
Inc.; page 8 (top right), (bottom right) © DigitalVision/PictureQuest © Photodisc
Green/Getty Images; page 9 (bkgd) © Lafi/Corbis; page 10 (bottom)
© M. L. Sinibaldi/Corbis; page 11 (bkgd) © Cindy Kassab/Corbis; page 12
(middle) © The Mazer Corporation, (bottom left) © ImageSource/ImageState,
(bottom middle) © Creatas, (bottom right) © KentKnudson/PhotoLink/Photodisc/
PictureQuest; page13 © The Mazer Corporation; page 14 (bkgd) © Ed
Bock/Corbis; page 15 (top right) © RJ Photo/Bruce Coleman, Inc., (bottom right)
© Rommel/Masterfile; page 16 (top) © The Mazer Corporation; page 17 (bkgd)
© Graham French/Masterfile; page 18 (bottom) © Stone/Getty Images; page 19
(bottom right) © University of Chicago, (top right) © Annie Griffiths Belt/Corbis;
page 20 (bkgd) © NOVASTOCK/PhotoEdit, Inc.; page 21 (middle right) © Rob
Crandall/Stock Boston, Inc./PictureQuest, (bkgd) © Royalty-Free/Corbis; page 22
(middle right) © NASA; page 23 (top) © The Mazer Corporation; page 24 (top
right) © Corbis, (bottom left) © PhotoDisc Green/Getty Images; page 25 (top
middle) © John Shaw/Bruce Coleman, Inc., (bottom middle) © Myrleen
Ferguson Cate/PhotoEdit, Inc.; pages 26-27 © The Mazer Corporation; pages
28-29 © Matt Meadows/Matt Meadows Photography; page 30 (bottom right)
© David-Young Wolf/PhotoEdit, Inc.

Neither the publisher nor the author shall be liable for any damage that may be
caused or sustained or result from conducting any of the activities in this book
without specifically following instructions, undertaking the activities without
proper supervision, or failing to comply with the cautions contained in the book.

Produced through the worldwide resources of the National Geographic Society,
John M. Fahey, Jr., President and Chief Executive Officer; Gilbert M. Grosvenor,
Chairman of the Board; Nina D. Hoffman, Executive Vice President and
President, Books and Education Publishing Group.

PREPARED BY NATIONAL GEOGRAPHIC SCHOOL PUBLISHING
Ericka Markman, Senior Vice President and President, Children's Books and
Education Publishing Group; Steve Mico, Vice President, Editorial Director;
Rosemary Baker, Executive Editor; Barbara Seeber, Editorial Manager; Jim
Hiscott, Design Manager; Kristin Hanneman, Illustrations Manager; Matt
Wascavage, Manager of Publishing Services; Sean Philpotts, Production
Coordinator.

MANUFACTURING AND QUALITY MANAGEMENT
Christopher A. Liedel, Chief Financial Officer; Phillip L. Schlosser, Director;
Clifton M. Brown, Manager.

PROGRAM DEVELOPER
Kate Boehm Jerome

ART DIRECTION
Daniel Banks, Project Design Company

CONSULTANT/REVIEWER
Dr. Timothy Cooney, Professor of Earth Science and Science Education,
University of Northern Iowa

BOOK DEVELOPMENT
The Mazer Corporation

Copyright © 2004 National Geographic Society. All Rights Reserved.
Reproduction in whole or in part of the contents without written permission from
the publisher is prohibited.

National Geographic Society, National Geographic School Publishing, National
Geographic Reading Expeditions, and the Yellow Border are trademarks of the
National Geographic Society.

Published by the National Geographic Society
1145 17th Street, N.W.
Washington, D.C. 20036-4688

ISBN-13: 978-0-7922-4800-2
ISBN-10: 0-7922-4800-7

Sixth Printing, January 2013
Printed in Canada

Contents

Weather Watch

A thunderstorm

The sky can be a busy place during a storm. Lightning flashes. Thunder rumbles. Clouds swirl. Yet all of this flashing and rumbling and swirling won't last long.

One day the sky can be a dark and stormy place. The next day—perhaps even the next hour—it can be clear, blue, and bright.

People have looked up into the sky for thousands of years, watching the weather and wondering why. Why, for example, did that lightning just flash across the sky? Long ago, the Greeks thought a god must be tossing lightning bolts from cloud to cloud.

People also watched the sky for clues and signs. They saw, for example, a ring around the moon and connected it with rain. They believed a red sunset meant the next day would be clear. Some of the beliefs were silly, but others turned out to be true.

This is a book about weather. Read on. You'll see what's causing the weather you're having right now. You'll also find out why you may have different weather tomorrow.

Chapter 1

Elements of Weather

It's All Up in the Air

Heated air in these
balloons makes them rise.

What's the weather where you are today? At the balloon festival there's a bright blue sky and a warm breeze. Huge balloons are floating up in the air.

Air is invisible. You can see right through it. But that doesn't mean it's not there. Air is all around us, and it has some very special qualities. These qualities cause the wind to blow. They make the weather change. They can even lift a huge balloon up, up, and away.

Air Is a Gas

Air is made up of tiny particles so small that you can't even see them. These particles have lots of energy. They move freely and bounce off each other. That makes air a gas.

The gas particles in the air also make the sky blue. Sunlight has all the colors of the rainbow. When sunlight strikes the particles, they reflect the color blue. And so the color blue is what you see.

Air Has Weight

Particles of air are tiny. However, the layer of air around Earth goes up for miles and miles. When you put all of those particles of air together, they have a lot of weight. The weight of the air is called **air pressure.**

Air pressure is not the same everywhere on Earth. In some spots, air pressure is high. That means the air is heavier.

In other spots, air pressure is low. There are fewer particles, with more space to spread apart. The air is lighter.

We can measure air pressure with a tool called a **barometer.** A barometer tells you whether the air pressure is high or low and whether it has changed.

A barometer measures air pressure.

Air Moves

Air particles are constantly moving. You don't usually feel this movement. But when lots of air particles move together from one spot to another, you do feel it. We call it wind.

What causes air to move from one place to another? Differences in air pressure make air move. Air moves from areas of higher pressure to areas of lower pressure.

You can see how this works if you blow up a long, skinny balloon part of the way and then pinch the opening closed. All of the air particles in the balloon are under the same pressure.

What would happen if you pressed down on one end of the balloon? That end would be under higher pressure. So some of the air particles would move to the other end where air pressure is lower.

What would happen if you let go of the balloon's open end? *Whoooosh!* The air particles would rush out. That's because air pressure outside the balloon was lower than inside.

Air particles are moving on a windy day.

Air Has Temperature

Is it warm outside today?

The sun shines on Earth and heats it. Then Earth warms the air above it. We measure the temperature of the air with a tool called a **thermometer.**

Warm air has more energy than cooler air. In warm air, the particles move faster. They spread farther apart. So warm air is lighter than cool air—and it rises.

Cool air has less energy than warm air. In cool air, the particles slow down. They stay closer together. For that reason, cool air is heavier than warm air. It sinks down toward the ground.

Why does a hot-air balloon float? How does it land?

The movement of air is wind. Wind has a lot of energy. In some windy places, people build windmills to capture that energy and turn it into electricity.

Air and Water Mix

Have you ever heard someone complain that it was hot and humid? Or cold and damp? Humid and damp describe another quality of air. They describe how wet the air feels to people.

The air feels humid or damp when there is water in it. You can't always see the water. Like air particles, water particles can be so small that you can't see them. Yet they are there in the air, mixed in with the air particles. When water is a gas in the air, it is called **water vapor.**

There can be more water vapor in warm air than in cool air. When the temperature gets cooler, some water vapor begins to change. The water particles start to slow down and come together. They form water droplets—bigger than gas particles, but still quite tiny. We call this **condensation.**

Do you want to see condensation? Then look for a cloud in the sky. A **cloud** is water that has condensed into droplets or tiny pieces of ice called ice crystals.

Did you ever wonder...

... what fog is?

Usually clouds form up in the sky. Sometimes a cloud forms in cool air moving over wet ground. That's one way fog forms. Fog is a cloud near the ground.

Look Out Below!

Sometimes many water droplets or ice crystals stick together, grow heavy—and fall. Water that falls from the sky is **precipitation.** Depending on the temperature of the air below or inside the cloud, the precipitation might be rain or snow or hail or sleet.

But how does water get into the sky in the first place? Sunlight gives the water on Earth energy. That water could be in the ocean, on the ground, or even on you. Energy turns the water into water vapor. We call this action **evaporation.** The water vapor rises into the sky, cools, condenses, and falls again. This is called the **water cycle.**

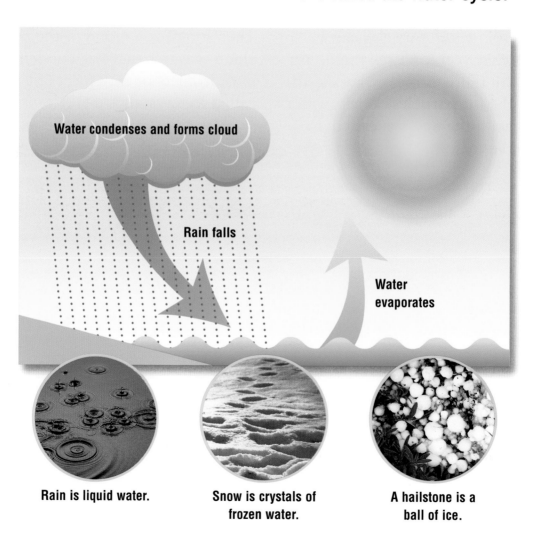

Water condenses and forms cloud

Rain falls

Water evaporates

Rain is liquid water.

Snow is crystals of frozen water.

A hailstone is a ball of ice.

When scientists **measure**, they find the size, the weight, or the amount of something. Measuring gives scientists data, or information. The information tells them what happened or what is happening. Scientists can also use the data to predict what will happen.

Rainfall can be measured with a **rain gauge.** A rain gauge collects rain. It has lines marked that tell how many inches of rain fell.

Look at the rain gauges. Each one shows the amount of rain that fell on a certain day.

On March 3, how much rain fell? On March 2, how much rain fell? Was it a quarter inch, a half inch, or more? Why does the rain gauge have to be emptied each day?

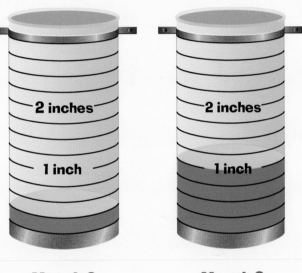

March 2   March 3

Add It All Together, You Get Weather

Suppose someone asked you what the weather is right now. What would you say?

You could tell whether it is sunny or cloudy or windy. You could say whether it is raining or snowing.

You might say, "It's too hot" (or too cold). You might tell whether it's humid, or "sticky," outside. You would be describing temperature, wind, and precipitation. All together, these conditions make up the weather.

Chapter 2

Moving Air Masses

A Change in the Weather

The day started warm and sunny.
What happened to change things?

Each day, the temperature, wind, and water in the air make up the weather. But the weather doesn't stay the same from day to day—or even for one day! Weather changes because the air moves. And the air is not the same everywhere.

Air Masses

Air masses roam over Earth's surface. Each air mass takes on the temperature of the surface below it. An air mass is huge. It can be hundreds of miles wide. It takes time—sometimes days—for it to move. In the meantime, it brings its own temperature and water—its own weather—with it.

Suppose an air mass from the North Pole moves south over a warmer area. Then it will bring cold, dry weather until it slowly gets warmer itself. Suppose an air mass over a warm ocean moves onto land. Then it will bring warm, humid weather until it slowly cools and dries out.

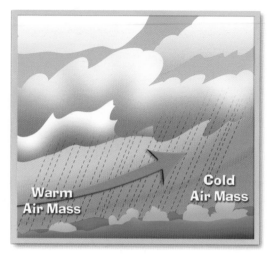

Warm Front

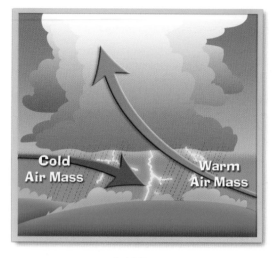

Cold Front

The Battle in the Sky

In the early 1900s, a team of scientists in Norway made some important observations about air masses. The team saw that changes in the weather happen along narrow zones where air masses meet. On one side of a zone, the temperature is warmer. On the other side of that zone, the temperature is cooler.

The team compared a change in weather to a battle between warm air and cold air. They called this zone a **front**, just like the line of fighting between two sides in a battle. Often precipitation falls along a front. Sometimes wind blows, too. After the front passes, the weather is different.

Air masses usually move over Earth's surface at different speeds and in different directions. This means that sooner or later one air mass will push into another one. When that happens, the front is named for the air mass that does the pushing. For example, when a cold air mass pushes into a warm air mass, a cold front forms. When a warm air mass pushes into a cold air mass, a warm front forms. Sometimes violent weather happens when two air masses meet at a front.

Thunderstorms

A thunderstorm can happen at a warm or a cold front. When cold air rams into warm air, the warm air is forced up. It cools, and its water vapor condenses. Huge clouds pile up, towering over the land below. Soon the rain comes pouring down. But that's not all. There is also electrical energy in a thunderstorm. This electrical energy flashes across the sky as lightning. Lightning can spark inside a cloud. It can leap from cloud to cloud. It can also streak between a cloud and Earth.

Lightning is powerful and superhot. It heats the air particles around it and sends them crashing into other air particles. These particles begin to shake, or vibrate. When this happens, you hear thunder.

A thunderstorm forms when cool air meets very warm, wet air.

Tornadoes

Sometimes another storm forms from a thunderstorm. A funnel cloud, shaped like a cone, may drop down out of a thunderstorm cloud. If its tip touches the ground, it becomes a **tornado**.

A tornado is a powerful twisting wind. Inside a tornado, the air pressure is very, very low. Winds spin rapidly around this tall column of low pressure.

A tornado may look black. But the air is not dark. It is still invisible.

You see the water droplets of the funnel cloud. You might also see dust and dirt and other material that the spinning winds have picked up. A tornado is so powerful that it can pick up animals and cars and uproot trees.

Hurricanes

The most powerful storm on Earth is a **hurricane**. A hurricane begins over the ocean. It gets its energy from the warm ocean water. This water evaporates into the air. The warm, wet air rises, and thunderstorms form.

Low air pressure inside a tornado sucks up the air—and anything else—around it.

A hurricane is a monster storm. If it hits land, look out. A wall of water crashes onto the shore. Then winds that are racing at more than 119 kilometers per hour (74 miles per hour) hit the shore. The rain from a hurricane can flood the land.

Seasons Bring Weather Changes

The weather can change from day to day. It can even change in a single day. Weather also changes slowly from week to week and month to month. Each season brings its own kind of weather.

Hurricanes form over oceans, but sometimes they strike the land.

Seasons occur as Earth moves around the sun each year. The part of Earth that is experiencing summer receives more energy from the sun. This energy causes warmer temperatures. The part of Earth that is experiencing winter receives less energy. Temperatures are cooler. The energy of the sun makes weather on Earth.

Focus On Tetsuya Fujita: Storm Expert

Tetsuya Fujita was fascinated by wind. As a scientist, he studied the damage caused by hurricanes and windstorms around the world. He was especially interested in tornadoes. Fujita made a scale that ranks a tornado on the damage it causes. He also invented a famous Tornado Machine. The machine creates tiny tornadoes to study. Thanks to Tetsuya Fujita, we have a clearer understanding of how tornadoes form.

Chapter 3

Predicting the Weather

What Will It Be Like Tomorrow?

A hurricane seen from space

High above us, in the darkness and silence of space, satellites orbit Earth. Satellites give weather forecasters information that help us know what to expect tomorrow.

You know what the weather was yesterday. You know what it is now. What will it be tomorrow? Or even a few hours from now?

It's helpful to know what weather changes will bring. To find out, you can watch the weather forecast on TV. The weather forecaster can tell you what the weather will probably be tomorrow. You can even find out what it will likely be a few days from now. How does the weather forecaster know?

Meteorologist checking satellite data

The weather forecaster studies the weather. The study of weather is **meteorology.** The scientists who study it are called **meteorologists.**

Meteorologists measure temperature, air pressure, wind, and precipitation. They use many tools to collect this weather data, including high-tech tools like satellites. Meteorologists study the data to figure out what causes weather changes.

Collecting Weather Data

A weather satellite helps gather data and sends the information back to Earth. It takes special pictures as it orbits high above Earth.

The air rises for miles and miles above Earth's surface. Different air conditions occur at different heights, which we call layers. All the layers of air together make up Earth's **atmosphere**.

The bottom layer of the atmosphere is 10–16 kilometers (6–10 miles) thick and is called the **troposphere**. *Tropos* comes from a Greek word meaning "change." The troposphere is also called the weather layer. That's because this layer is where weather occurs.

Some weather satellites orbit Earth near the top of the upper layer of the atmosphere. Others travel even beyond that, into space. A satellite can show clouds and storms in the troposphere. A satellite also gathers information about the land and water temperatures on Earth. That's because those temperatures can change the air above.

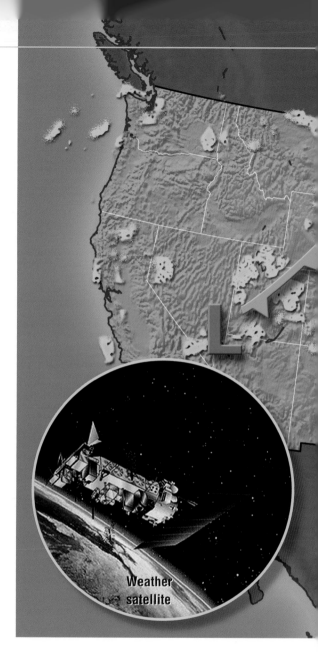

Weather satellite

Making a Forecast

Besides using weather satellites, meteorologists also launch weather balloons into the troposphere. These balloons measure air pressure and other conditions. **Radar** can help meteorologists to track storms and precipitation.

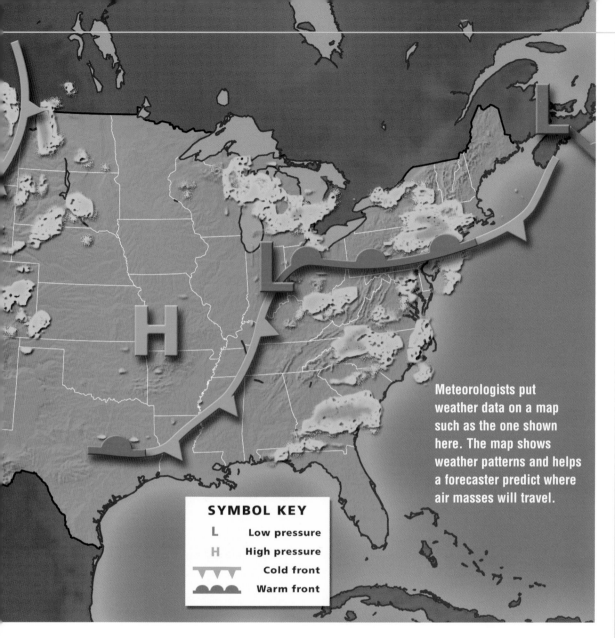

Meteorologists put weather data on a map such as the one shown here. The map shows weather patterns and helps a forecaster predict where air masses will travel.

SYMBOL KEY

L — Low pressure
H — High pressure
— Cold front
— Warm front

Meteorologists work at weather stations around the country. They use these tools to record the weather data where they are. All this information is fed into computers. It is shared with all the other weather stations.

Using this up-to-the-minute data, meteorologists can draw maps of air masses and fronts. They use their knowledge of weather patterns to answer the question, "What will the weather be tomorrow?"

Clues in the Clouds

You know clouds have different shapes. But did you know that the shape of a cloud may give you a clue to the weather?

Cumulus

Cumulus clouds are fair weather clouds. They are the puffy, white clouds you see floating across the sky when the weather is calm and dry.

Stratus

Stratus clouds are low, flat clouds. They cover the sky like a gray sheet. Look for precipitation when you see stratus clouds.

Cirrus

Cirrus clouds are high, wispy clouds. They are made of ice crystals. Cirrus clouds may signal a change in the weather.

Cumulonimbus

Cumulonimbus clouds pile up high in the sky. At the bottom, they are often dark gray. Look for thunderstorms when you see cumulonimbus clouds.

Thinking Like a Scientist

Measuring

Measuring is an important skill. You measure when you stand on a scale to weigh yourself. You measure when you stand against a chart to see how tall you are.

Measuring gives scientists data—numbers they can study and use. Scientists use data to understand what has happened. They also use data to predict what will happen.

One thing scientists measure is the speed of the wind. They use an **anemometer** to measure it. An anemometer has cups that catch the wind. The wind spins the cups around. The number of times they spin in a minute tells you how fast the wind is blowing. A gauge on the anemometer counts the spins and records the speed.

Practice the Skill

Look at each anemometer below. How fast is the wind blowing in each picture?

Check It Out

The Beaufort Scale describes the effects of wind speeds. The scale describes the effects that each wind speed has. Look on page 27 to see the Beaufort Scale and the wind speeds the scale can measure. Then look again at the pictures below and see where those wind speeds fall on the Beaufort Scale. What kinds of winds do the anemometers measure?

Beaufort Scale

	Name	Miles per hour	Effect
0	Calm	Under 1	No effect
1	Light air	1–3	Smoke drifts
2	Light breeze	4–7	Wind vane moves; leaves rustle; smoke blows
3	Gentle breeze	8–12	Flags and leaves and twigs move
4	Moderate breeze	13–18	Loose papers blow; small branches sway
5	Fresh breeze	19–24	Small trees sway
6	Strong breeze	25–31	Large branches sway; umbrellas hard to use
7	Moderate gale	32–38	Whole trees sway; hard to walk into wind
8	Fresh gale	39–46	Twigs break off trees
9	Strong gale	47–54	Slight damage to buildings; roof may blow off
10	Whole gale	55–63	Trees break or are uprooted; buildings damaged
11	Storm	64–74	Cars overturned
12	Hurricane	75 and up	Great destruction; buildings destroyed

How Hot Is It?

When the sun's energy strikes Earth, things heat up. We use a thermometer to measure the amount of heat something has. A thermometer may measure heat in degrees Fahrenheit (°F) or degrees Celsius (°C). Some thermometers show both ways to measure heat.

Not all things take in heat the same way. Some things heat up more slowly. Some cool off more quickly. See for yourself how soil, or dirt, and water heat differently.

Materials
- ✔ 2 jars, the same size
- ✔ Soil
- ✔ Water
- ✔ Thermometer

Explore

1 Let the soil and water sit overnight in a room. The soil and water should be at room temperature when you start this activity.

2 Fill one jar with the soil.

3 Fill the second jar with the water.

4 Place both jars in a sunny spot for one hour.

5 After one hour, put the thermometer in the water. Wait one minute. Record the temperature.

6 Wipe off the thermometer, and put it in the jar of soil. Wait one minute. Record the temperature.

Hint: You probably found that the soil was warmer than the water. Land heats up more quickly than water.

7 Put the jars in a shady place for one hour. Then repeat steps 5 and 6.

Hint: You probably found that the soil was cooler than the water. Land loses heat more quickly than water.

Think

At the seashore, would the air over the land be cooler or warmer than the air over the water one hour after sunrise? Would the air over the land be cooler or warmer than the air over the water one hour after sunset?

Science Notebook

WILD WEATHER FACTS

- The hottest temperature ever measured on Earth was in Libya in Africa. On September 13, 1922, the thermometer read 58°C (136°F).
- The hottest temperature ever measured in the United States was in Death Valley, California. On July 10, 1913, it was 57°C (134°F).

BOOKS TO READ

There are many books about the weather. Some explain how the weather happens. Others show how to make weather models. Check your school or local library. Here are just a few:

Adams, Simon. *The Best Book of Weather.* Kingfisher Publications, 2001.

Farndon, John. *Weather* (in Science Experiments series). Benchmark Books, Marshall Cavendish, 2001.

Llewellyn, Claire. *Wild, Wet, and Windy.* Candlewick Press, 1997.

WEBSITES TO VISIT

Here are some websites with more information, activities, and links.

National Weather Service:
http://nws.noaa.gov/om/reachout/kidspage.shtml

The Weather Dude:
www.wxdude.com

Web Weather for Kids:
www.ucar.edu/40th/webweather

Glossary

air mass – air that takes on the temperature and water of the land it is over

air pressure – the weight of the air

anemometer (*an-uh-MAH-muh-tur*) – a tool to measure wind speed

atmosphere (*AT-mus-feer*) – the layers of air that surround Earth

barometer (*buh-RAH-muh-tur*) – a tool to measure air pressure

cloud – water vapor that has condensed into droplets in the sky

condensation (*kahn-den-SAY-shun*) – the action of water vapor cooling and turning to water

evaporation (*i-vap-uh-RAY-shun*) – the action of water warming up and turning to water vapor

front – the zone where a cold air mass and warm air mass meet

hurricane – a storm with high winds and rainfall that forms over the ocean

measure – to find the size, weight, or amount of something

meteorologist (*mee-tee-uh-RAHL-uh-jist*) – a scientist who studies weather

meteorology (*mee-tee-uh-RAHL-uh-jee*) – the study of weather

precipitation (*pree-sip-uh-TAY-shun*) – water falling from the sky in the form of rain, snow, hail, or sleet

radar – device that uses radio waves to find position and speed

rain gauge – a tool to measure the amount of rainfall

thermometer (*thur-MAH-muh-tur*) – a tool to measure temperature

tornado – a violent, twisting windstorm, in the shape of a funnel, that forms from a thunderstorm cloud

troposphere (*TROH-puh-sfeer*) – the layer of air closest to Earth's surface; the weather layer

water cycle – natural cycle that moves water between Earth's surface and atmosphere through evaporation, condensation, and precipitation

water vapor – water in the form of a gas

Index